5-8

Easy-to-make
Puppets

Easy-to-make Puppets

JOYCE LUCKIN

photographs by
Livia Rolandini

Publishers **PLAYS, INC.** Boston

With grateful thanks
to my husband
for his encouragement

First published in Great Britain 1975
by GEORGE G. HARRAP & CO. LTD, LONDON

First American edition published by
PLAYS, INC. 1975

Library of Congress Cataloging in Publication Data

Luckin, Joyce.
Easy-to-make puppets.

SUMMARY: Instructions, patterns, and photographs
reveal how to create twenty-four puppets—hand, glove,
and marionette.

1. Puppet making—Juvenile literature. (1. Puppets
and puppet-plays) I. Title.

TT184.7.L8 1975   745.59'22   74–17063

ISBN 0–8238–0178–0

Printed in Great Britain

CONTENTS

INTRODUCTION

Puppets are an excellent source for the imaginative power of the child, enabling him to create a world of fantasy. Puppets can bring to life little people, animals and even objects.

Any scraps of fabric can be used; never throw anything away. Most of the puppets in this book are made from felt because it is colourful, easy to handle and does not fray, but they can all be made equally well from any scraps of bright material. (If a turning on the material is necessary, do not forget to cut out the pattern just a little bigger to allow for this.) The patterns are drawn out on squared pages. All you have to do is copy them exactly onto paper with 2 cm squares (graph paper will do).

Children like to identify with the puppets and should be encouraged to invent stories and plays around their puppets. I have included a couple of my own stories in this book. Even if you do not wish to use them they may inspire you.

Children are not interested in exact imitation; their own drawings show this. A simple puppet will excite them and encourage them to make use of their own imaginative powers. Before now, we have painted faces on paper bags, stuffed them with newspaper and added a cardboard tube for easy handling and found that these simple creations have kept children from four to seven years old amused for quite long periods; they have quite happily added their own words to the actions of the puppets they are manipulating, and thoroughly enjoyed doing so.

To make the puppets more interesting and colourful I have decorated them but they can be very successful without decoration. I have only briefly suggested colours as it is much better to use whatever is available, plus a bit of imagination. It is a good idea to make the puppets with whatever you have to hand rather than waiting until a certain material or colour is obtainable, as often inspiration wanes. Individuality is very important: my ideas are only offered as guides, but I hope they will encourage you to develop your ideas in whatever way suits your own particular needs, and the interests of the children with whom you are working. If Little Johnnie has a fixation with worms, then make him a colourful worm which can be manipulated by his tiny hands and he will be delighted.

Of course, colours are also important and you will have your own ideas on this subject. White easily becomes grubby so, from a practical point of view, I use it sparingly.

Besides making puppets of animals and people I also like to make shape puppets; this is useful in introducing these new concepts to young children. Therefore, I have added a cube, a star, an oblong and a diamond to this collection. I have also included Punch and Judy, as they often symbolize puppets for children. There are three marionettes also as these are a more sophisticated form of puppetry and are very much enjoyed by slightly older children. Young children will love the mouth puppets which are very expressive and easy to manipulate. All these have been used with young children and have proved to be great favourites. I sew a curtain ring onto the back of the hand puppets and then hang the puppets on the classroom wall with their names printed clearly underneath.

I hope that you will enjoy making and using this selection of puppets and that they will fire your imagination to make many others of your own.

JOYCE LUCKIN

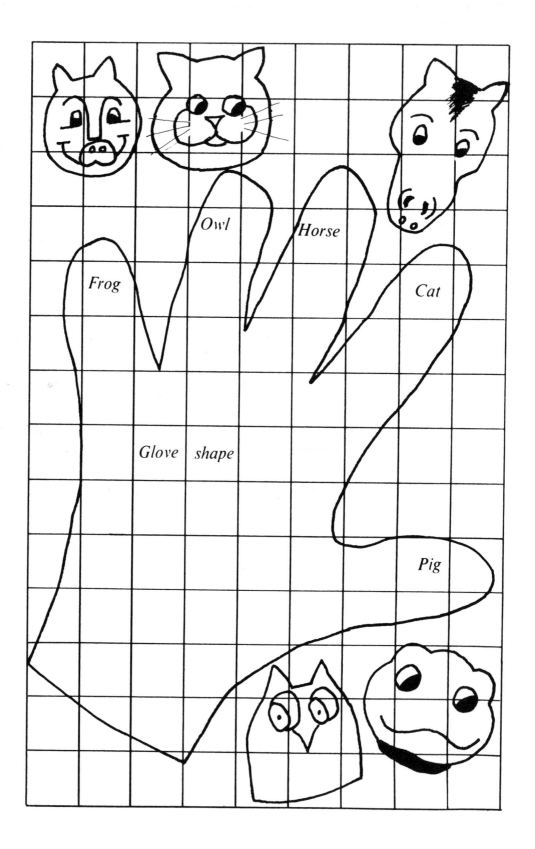

Owl

Horse

Frog

Cat

Glove shape

Pig

FINGER PUPPET

Materials

*A piece of felt large enough to make a glove
to fit your hand in flesh pink or fawn
Small pieces of felt in various colours
Embroidery cottons and a few sequins*

Method

Put your hand on a sheet of paper and draw round it leaving ample room for a loose fitting glove (say about $\frac{1}{2}$ cm all round). The glove in the diagram is for an average-sized adult. Cut two pieces of felt in this shape and oversew all the edge except the cuff. Trace each animal face from the diagram and enlarge it to cover amply the finger on which it is going to be sewn. (NB. Decide which hand you wish to have the glove puppet on and sew the animal faces on the correct side of the glove.)

Pig   Make him a pink face with green eyes, darker pink features and French knots for his nose.

Cat   Make her out of white, grey or ginger felt. Add green or blue eyes, a pink nose and mouth and black features. Use stiff nylon for the whiskers.

Horse   Make him from brown felt with blue or brown eyes, fawn features and use fawn wool for the mane.

Owl   Make him from light fawn felt with green sequin eyes and bright yellow features.

Frog   Make in green felt with black eyes either embroidered in or using black beads and black features.

When each animal face is made sew it onto the appropriate finger of the felt glove. These faces should be put on in the same order as shown in the diagram, as they are used in the story of Klintoch the Clown. If you find you cannot hold up the fingers with the horse and owl heads on easily, try holding the other fingers down with the thumb.

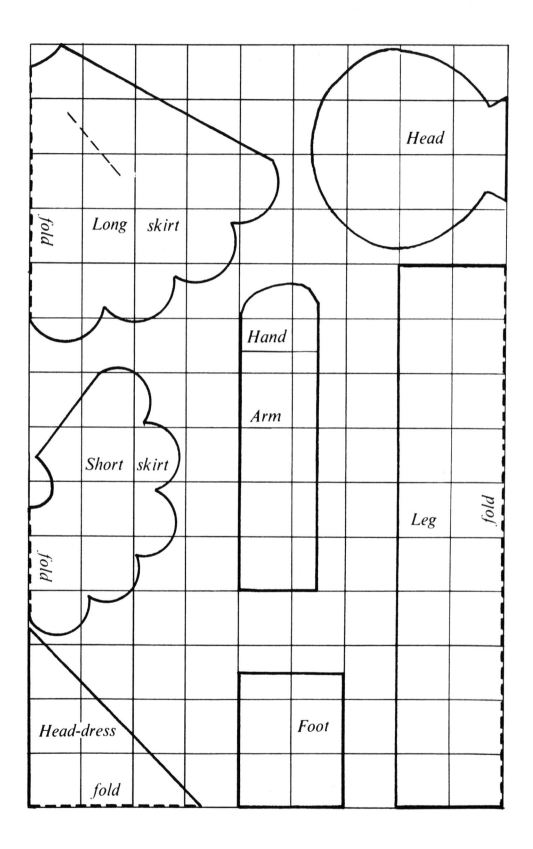

FUCHSIA FAIRY

Materials

Fuchsia pink felt for long skirt
Mauve felt for head-dress and short skirt
Flesh pink felt for face and legs
Scraps of pink or mauve felt for shoes
Embroidery threads to match pink and mauve
Sequins and beads for decoration
Artificial hair or fine wool for hair
Oddments of felt for face features
Kapok or suitable material for stuffing

Method

Cut a long skirt in fuschia pink as shown in diagram, placing on a fold of material. Use blanket stitch in mauve embroidery cotton to match the short skirt and decorate edge. Trim with gold sequins. Sew up the long seam of the long skirt, making a cone shape. Cut a short skirt in mauve felt placing on a fold of material. Decorate with embroidery in pink to match the long skirt and trim with French knots and small beads.

Cut two arms and sew the long seam and the rounded edge of the hand. Stuff hand and sew stuffing into position. Leave straight edge open and sew front side of straight edge onto long skirt where shown by dotted lines. Leave back of straight edge open for insertion of thumb and little finger for manipulation of puppet.

Cut two legs in flesh pink and sew long seam. Cut two feet in pink or mauve felt and folding in half sew onto ends of legs. Sew legs into position under long skirt and fasten firmly at neck edge.

Cut two heads in flesh pink and with felt mark in the face features. Place a strip of hair around the face coming down about 2.5 cm over the short skirt. When hair is in position, stick on. Cut one head-dress in felt to match short skirt. Trim edge with embroidery thread to match the long skirt, using herringbone or similar stitch, and trim with sequins or beads. Sew head-dress onto head with the trimmed edge framing the face, and fasten at the back of the head with tiny stitches, or stick with adhesive. Sew neck onto skirt and then place short skirt over long skirt and trim to fit neck; neatly sew onto neck on the wrong side. Sew the back seam of the short skirt.

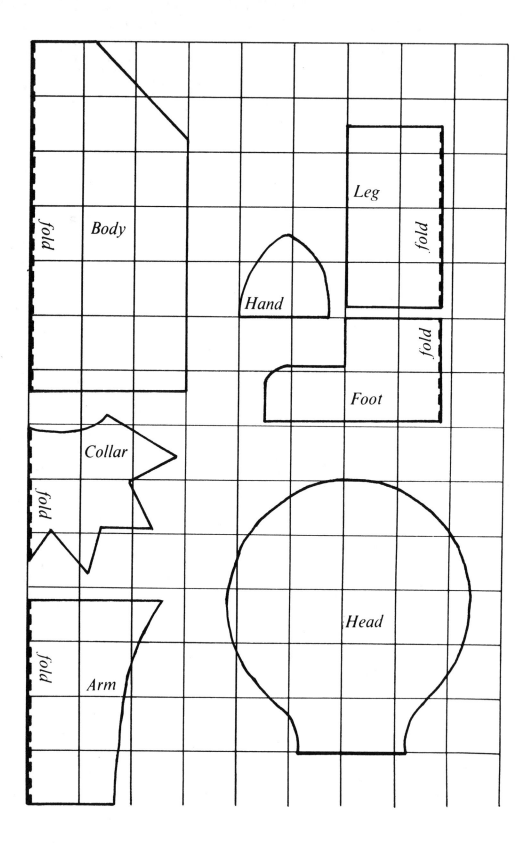

MO THE ESKIMO

Materials

Turquoise felt for body, arms and legs
Flesh coloured felt for face and hands
Purple felt for trimming
White fur for trimming head
Red felt for shoes
Embroidery thread for decoration
Black wool for hair
Embroidery thread for face features
Kapok or old nylon tights for stuffing

Method

Cut two pieces of turquoise felt for the body. Sew the underarm seams and decorate the bottom edge of the body with purple felt embellished with embroidery thread in red, blue, yellow, green and mauve. Cut two arms in felt to match the body. Trim the edge to match the edge of the body, and sew into position on armhole. Cut out four hands. Sew round the curved edge and then sew onto wrists. These hands are not stuffed as they are used for manipulating the puppet. Cut two legs in felt to match body and trim to match edge of body and sleeves. Sew up seam and top edge (not trimmed edge) to body about 1.2 cm underneath front piece, sewing legs about 1.2 cm from the side seams and touching each other.

Cut out four feet in red felt and trim with two rows of herringbone stitch in contrasting colour. Sew seams and then stuff tightly; sew onto legs when you have stuffed the legs.

Cut two heads and embroider face features on front piece. Trim all round face with white fur. Sew the back of the head on. (This may be in black felt if desired.) Cut out collar and decorate with embroidery. Put around neck and sew on under the fur trimming at the front.

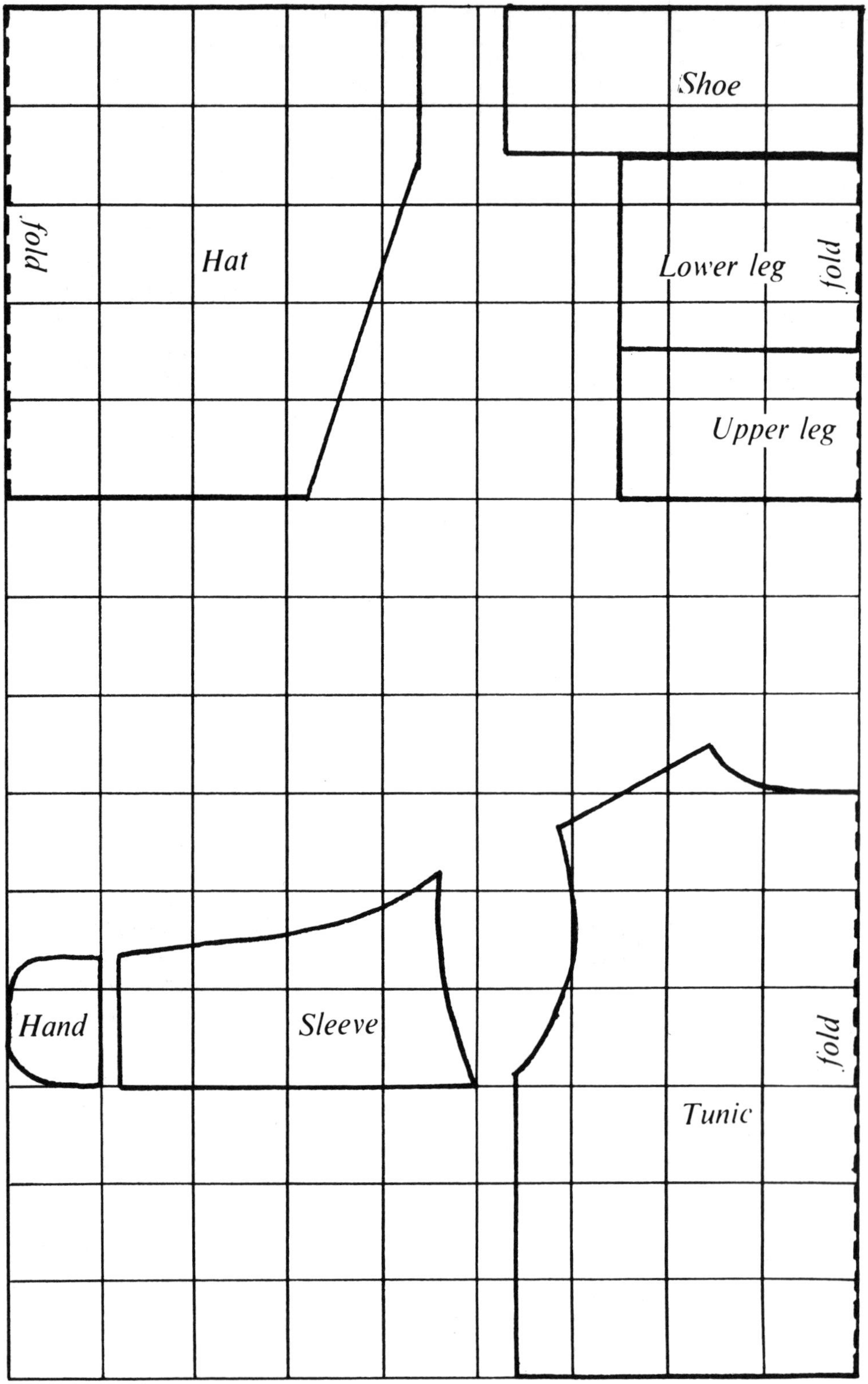

Shoe

fold

Hat

Lower leg

fold

Upper leg

Hand

Sleeve

fold

Tunic

EIKKY FROM FINLAND

Materials

Blue felt for tunic
Red felt for hat and trimming on tunic
Flesh coloured felt for face, hands and legs
Brown felt for boots
Silk flowered material for scarf
Yellow wool for hair
Oddments of embroidery cotton
Kapok or old nylon tights for stuffing

Method

Cut two pieces of blue felt for the tunic. Sew the side seams, trim the bottom with a strip of red felt 1.2 cm wide and decorate with a line of embroidery in yellow. Cut two sleeves in blue felt. Trim cuff with a strip of red felt .7 cm wide. Sew underarm seam and then sew into place on tunic. Trim seam with a strip of red felt .7 cm wide, also trim from the sleeve to the shoulder with narrow red felt.

Cut four hands in flesh coloured felt. Sew round the curved edge leaving the straight edge open. Sew onto the cuff of the sleeve. The sleeve and hand are left unstuffed to enable the little finger and thumb to be inserted to manipulate the puppet. Cut one circle in flesh coloured felt 7 cm in diameter. Embroider in face features. Cut strips of yellow wool and stick round face as hair. Cut red felt hat and decorate with embroidery in yellow and green using French knots, lazy daisy stitch and broken chain stitch. Sew embroidered edge of hat round face of puppet, arranging hair attractively. Join both seams and cut a narrow strip of red felt to be sewn under chin attached to hat, but neaten where head is sewn onto tunic in front and tunic is sewn to hat at the back.

Cut two upper legs in flesh coloured felt and two lower legs in brown. Sew a piece of each together and then join the side seam. Cut four shoes in brown felt. Join seams and sew onto brown portion of leg. Stuff leg and shoe securely and then sew onto tunic about 1.2 cm underneath front piece, about 1.2 cm from side seams placing both legs together.

Cut a 12 cm square of thin patterned material and whip the edges. Sew a fringe onto the edges of the scarf, made from embroidery thread. Fold cornerways and tie round neck of puppet, securing with a stitch.

15

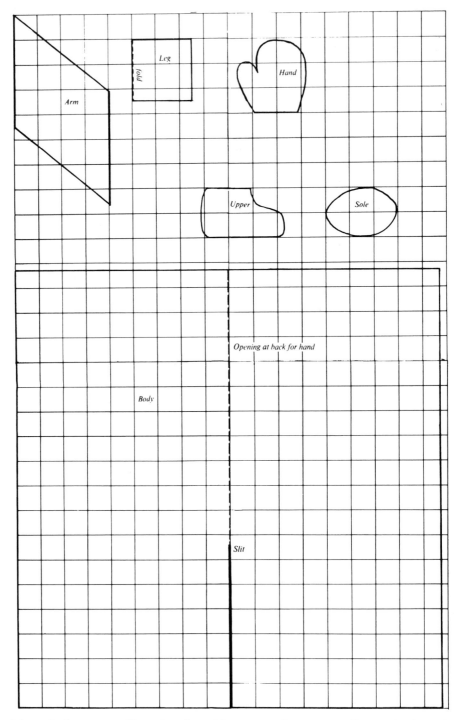

To avoid confusion you will notice that this pattern is on a smaller scale than the other designs, but the same principle holds good—you transfer the design onto 2 cm squared graph paper.

KLINTOCH THE CLOWN

Materials

Brightly patterned cotton about 46 cm × 92 cm
About 2 m of 2.5 cm white lace
Small piece of stiff material for the hat
Black wool for hair
Scraps of flesh pink felt for hands and legs
Pencil or dowelling for head support
Cotton or wooden ball 7.5 cm in diameter
Adhesive
Oddments of felt or soft leather for shoes
Scraps of red wool for pompom on top of hat
Kapok or old nylon tights for stuffing

Method

Cut the tunic from the cotton. Cut a slit for the legs and sew the seams. Gather at the ankle and trim with gathered lace. Sew the sleeve seams and gather at wrist, again trimming with gathered lace. Gather and trim neck with lace. Leave an opening at the back for the hand to manipulate puppet.

Cut four hands in flesh coloured felt. Sew all round curved edge leaving straight edge open. The gathered wrist of the tunic is then sewn onto this hand leaving room for a finger to go through to manipulate puppet. Cut two legs in flesh coloured felt and join short edge. Sew onto ankle of tunic ready for shoe to be joined.

Cut four uppers and two soles in felt or soft leather. Join uppers together and then sew onto sole. Stuff with kapok or suitable stuffing and sew onto the leg, when you have attached the leg to the tunic ankle. The top of the shoe must be sewn across to stop the stuffing from coming out.

Cut a circle of stiff material about 16 cm in diameter and fold it into a cone, sticking the straight edge then carefully fit the lower edge to the ball which is to be the head. With the red wool make a pompom and stick on the cone which forms the clown's hat. Take the ball and paint a happy face on one side and an unhappy face on the reverse, so that the head can be swivelled round to show either an unhappy or a happy face. Make a hole in the head and stick it securely onto a pencil; this gives the manipulator something to hold onto in order to swivel the face round to make it happy or sad. Stick the strands of black wool across the head to hang down each side of the face, then stick the hat on top.

A STORY ABOUT KLINTOCH THE CLOWN WHO LOST HIS SMILE

Klintoch was usually a very happy clown, but today he got up and discovered that his smile had disappeared. He looked under the bed, in the cupboard and even behind the television set, but he could not find his smile anywhere, and who wants a clown without a smile? Sadly he ate his breakfast and decided to search for his smile as quickly as he could.

He hurried out into the morning sunshine and set off down the road; he had a very important thing to do—to see if he could find his smile. He had not gone very far down the road when he came to the pond; as he stood and looked at his reflection in the pond he heard a croaking noise: it was Mr Frog.

'Oh, Mr Frog,' called out Klintoch. 'A dreadful thing has happened. When I got up this morning my smile had gone.'

'Well really!' said Mr Frog. 'Now, isn't that a horrible thing to happen. But really Klintoch I don't know what you think I can do about it, I'm busy rounding up my tadpoles. They seem to have swum away. So you see I am *awfully* busy.' And off he went into the pond with a splash.

'Well really!' thought Klintoch. 'People seem too busy to help anyone these days. I'd have helped him look for his tadpoles, if only I could have found my smile first.'

On went Klintoch until he came to the oak tree; he sat under it for a while and then, looking up at the sky through its branches, he spotted Mr Owl.

'Oh, hullo Mr Owl,' Klintoch called. 'Such a terrible thing has happened to me. I've lost my smile.'

'Have you now,' hooted Mr Owl. 'Some people are very careless it seems. Where did you lose it?'

'Well, if I knew I wouldn't be looking for it, would I?' replied Klintoch, a little cross at being asked such a silly question.

'I really don't know,' said Mr Owl. 'I'm feeling very sleepy; I usually sleep when it is light you know, but if you still haven't found your smile when it gets dark, I'll come and help you look for it.'

'Well, thank you,' called out Klintoch. 'I hope you have a nice sleep.' And he went on his way, leaving Mr Owl in peace.

When he got to the meadow he saw Mr Horse galloping around having a fine time.

'He seems to be enjoying himself,' grumbled Klintoch. So he climbed on the gate so that Mr Horse would see him. Mr Horse soon did and came galloping across because Klintoch just might have a juicy apple to give him to eat, and he did like juicy apples.

'Hullo!' called Mr Horse in a friendly manner.

'Hullo!' replied Klintoch. 'I'm sorry I've forgotten to bring you an apple, but you see, I've lost my smile and it has really put me out.'

'I quite understand,' said Mr Horse. 'It must be very inconvenient to be without a smile. Do you think you lost it in my field?'

'I really don't know,' said Klintoch, 'but if you would gallop around and look for me I'd be very obliged.'

'Of course I will,' said Mr Horse and galloped off.

Klintoch was really getting despondent now and he walked slowly down the road until he came to a cottage where Mrs Cat was sitting on the step washing her face.

'Hullo Klintoch, isn't it a lovely day?' called out Mrs Cat.

'It might be for you, but it isn't for me,' Klintoch replied. 'I've lost my smile and I feel very unhappy.'

'Oh, I can imagine what you must be feeling,' said Mrs Cat. 'That isn't a very nice thing to happen. I do hope you find it. I have my kittens to look for or I would help you to search for it.'

'Well, if you helped me I could help you look for your kittens,' said Klintoch. But he was too late. Mrs Cat had skipped off.

He felt he would never find his smile and was very miserable, when he heard a funny noise from the farmyard nearby. It wasn't the cluck-clucking of the hens, or the gentle mooing of the cows, or even the barking of the dog; he knew all those noises well, but this was quite different. He stopped and went over to the source of the sound. He couldn't believe his eyes; he stood and looked, and looked, and looked, and then suddenly without warning he started to laugh and he laughed, and laughed and laughed. Mrs Pig was startled by the noise and stopped grovelling.

'Whatever is the matter with you?' she asked.

'Well, I really must thank you,' said Klintoch. 'I'd lost my smile but seeing you I've found it again. I say, you do look funny—your nose is covered with dirt!'

'Really!' exclaimed Mrs Pig, who was not amused.

'Thank you all the same,' called out Klintoch as he hurried off to tell his friends.

He found Mrs Cat sunning herself; she had found her kittens and was happy.

'I've found my smile,' called Klintoch gaily as he tripped past her cottage.

'I'm so glad, and I've found my kittens. They were at the well,' she said proudly.

Klintoch reached the field where Mr Horse was still galloping around looking for his smile. He gave Mr Horse an apple that he had picked as he passed the cottage.

'I'm so pleased to see that you have found your smile,' said Mr Horse, happily munching the apple.

Klintoch decided not to wake Mr Owl as he passed the tree, so he left a note instead telling him that he had found his smile. He added some kisses as he was so pleased.

Back at the pond he found Mr Frog, who by now had all his tadpoles.

'I've found my smile,' said Klintoch, beaming.

'Yes, I can see,' croaked Mr Frog. 'But I don't know what all the fuss is for, I never smile at anyone and no-one ever seems to mind.'

Klintoch smiled to himself and went home for dinner. By now he was feeling very hungry and he was satisfied that he had found what he went out for.

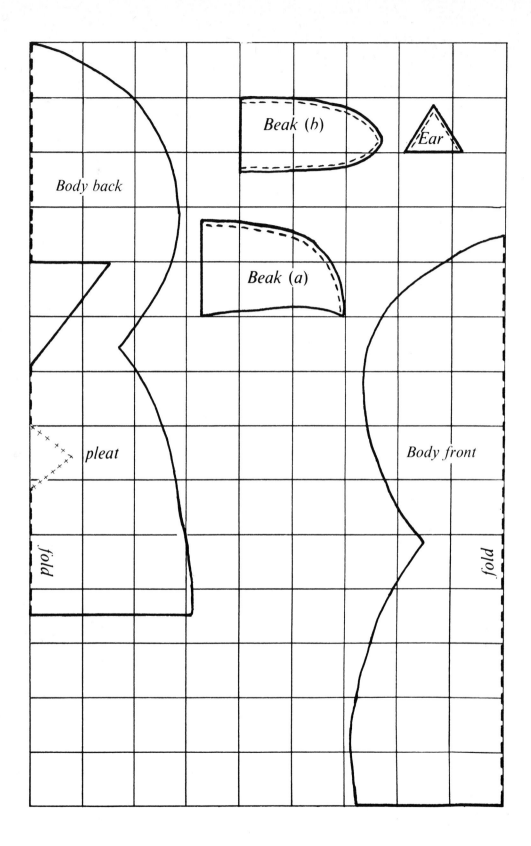

Body back

Beak (b)

Ear

Beak (a)

pleat

fold

Body front

fold

OLIVER OWL

Materials

Fawn felt for head and body
Scraps of white and light brown felt
2 black beads or buttons for inner eyes
Matching cottons

Method

Cut two pieces of beak (a) in light brown felt and three pieces of beak (b) in light brown felt. Join beak (a) where shown by dotted line. Join these to one piece of beak (b). Join the remaining pieces of beak (b) where shown. Now join together the piece of beak (b) in the upper beak to one piece from the lower beak.

Cut one back body and one front body. Halfway up the head of owl cut out shape to take both upper and lower beak and stitch the outer beak edges into position. Cut two circles of white felt 3cm in diameter and stitch onto front of head as outer eyes. Sew black beads into position as inner eyes.

Cut four pieces of ear in fawn felt. Stitch two pieces together as shown by dotted line. Repeat with other ear. Sew both ears into position at sides of top of head. Join back and front body together, making dart where shown.

The puppet is manipulated by inserting the thumb and first finger into the beak.

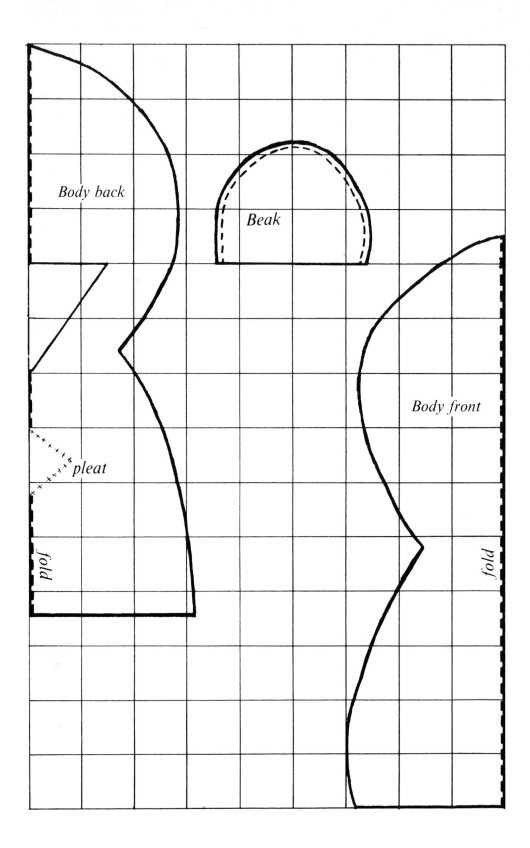

Body back

Beak

Body front

pleat

fold

fold

DESMOND DUCK

Materials

Yellow felt for head and body
Scraps of orange felt for beak
2 black beads or buttons for eyes
Matching cottons

Method

Cut four pieces of beak in orange. Join two pieces as indicated by dotted line. Join the other two pieces in the same way. Join the beak together by stitching the inner layers of felt of each beak. This leaves the two outer layers of felt to be stitched onto the head of the duck.

Cut one back body and one front body. In the front body two thirds of the way down from the top of the duck head cut an oval shape big enough to sew the two edges of the beak in. Stitch in securely on wrong side. Sew bead eyes into position. On wrong side join back to front, making dart where shown.

The puppet is manipulated by inserting the thumb and first finger into the beak.

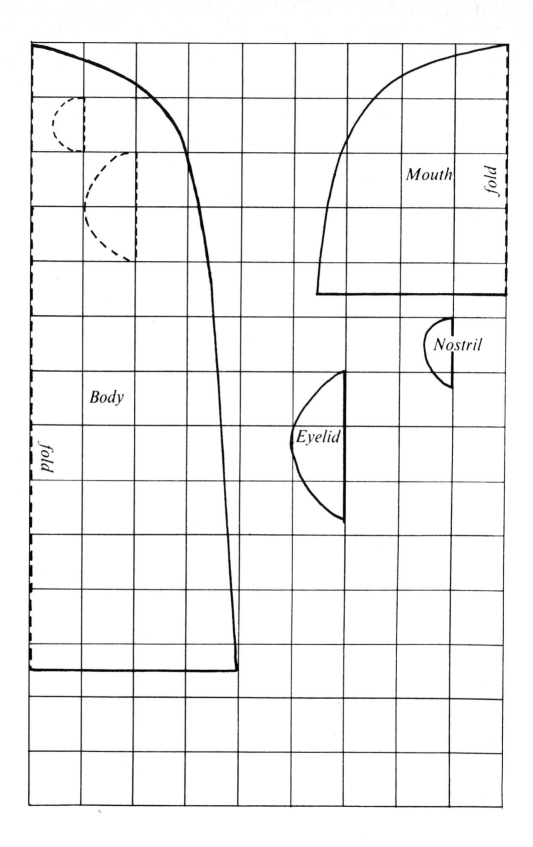

ALEXANDER ALLIGATOR

Materials

Dark green felt for head and body
Pink felt for mouth and nostrils
Round and bugle buttons
Matching cottons

Method

Cut two bodies in dark green felt. Cut two eyelids in dark green felt. Cut two pieces of pink felt for mouth as shown on body. Sew inner mouth into position on green body. Then join mouth along the straight edge, making a tuck in the pink felt to make it a better shape. Sew eyelids into position on face as indicated on diagram, sewing on curved edge.

Cut two nostrils in pink felt and stitch into position on head where indicated. Stitch sides of body together on the wrong side. Sew round white buttons about the size of a marble into eyelid sockets. Stitch white bugle beads upright as teeth in lower jaw of alligator, keeping them at the sides of the mouth.

The puppet is manipulated by inserting fingers in the top jaw and the thumb in the bottom jaw.

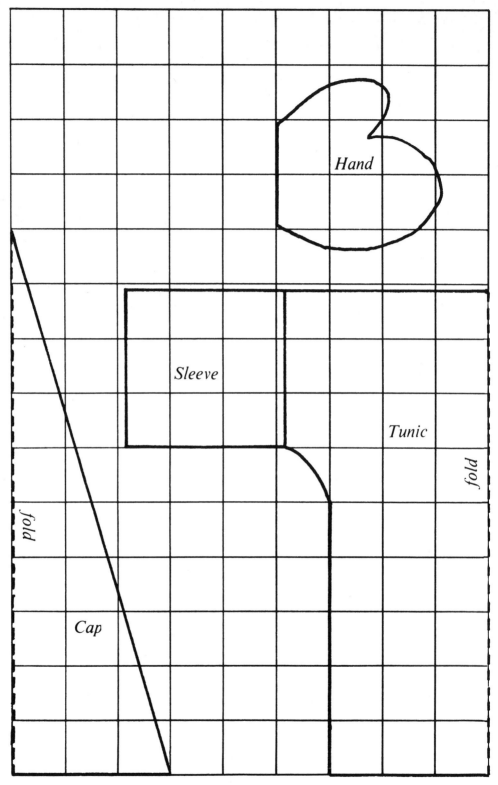

Hand

Sleeve

Tunic

fold

fold

Cap

PUNCH AND JUDY

Materials

Green felt for Punch's tunic
Blue felt for Judy's tunic
Oddments of felt
2 masks (as for marionettes)
White lawn for Judy's mob cap
2.5 cm wide lace for trimming

Method

PUNCH

Cut two pieces of tunic in green felt. Oversew shoulder and underarm seams. Cut two pieces of white felt for sleeves. Oversew short edge and then stitch into armhole on tunic. Gather at wrist to size of hand. Cut four hands in flesh pink felt. Sew to form hand and slightly stuff thumb and top of hand. Sew onto gathered wrist of sleeve, leaving room for finger to go through for easy manipulation.

Make mask as for marionette emphasizing nose, chin, cheek bones and eyebrows on mould with plasticine. When painting in features give Punch a red nose and chin, highly coloured cheekbones, prominent eyebrows and a laughing mouth. Back mask with pink felt and sew head onto tunic leaving room for fingers to go in. Neaten neck edge of mask to tunic with pink felt and trim with several rows of lace. There is no need for hair. Cut hat in red felt. Sew edge, catch point at the top to the back of the hat at the neck edge. Cut white felt trimming and stick hat onto head and cover join with trimming.

JUDY

Cut two pieces of tunic in blue felt. Oversew shoulder and underarm seams. Make sleeves and hands as given for Punch. Make mask as given for Punch.

Cut two pieces of white lawn in a circle 25 cm in diameter and stitch round outer edge, leaving room to turn material right side out and neaten the opening. Draw an inner circle 15 cm in diameter and draw this up to form a mob cap by making a line of running stitches. Stick cap onto Judy's head. (Again, there is no need for hair.) Cover stitching with a strip of felt to match tunic. Trim neck of tunic with a white felt collar or lace. If you require a baby for Judy make as given in the Nativity set and stitch or stick to Judy's right arm.

fold

Basic *shape*

To avoid confusion you will notice that this pattern is on a smaller scale than the other designs, but the same principle holds good—you transfer the design onto 2 cm squared graph paper.

28

NATIVITY GROUP

MARY
The basic shape should be in red, blue or white material and the design at the bottom a simple feminine one in pinks, blues and white. She has long dark hair and a simple veil of white lawn, topped by a veil of blue chiffon. The baby is made from pink material the size of a thumb, stuffed with kapok and with a face painted on. A little dark hair could be added before swathing the figure in white.

JOSEPH
The basic shape should be in brown felt or tweed material. He has long hair, a long full beard and a design of the straight line variety in greens, yellows and white on the bottom of the tunic. His head-dress is a piece of fine white linen with a band of gold or yellow braid just above the eyebrows. His tunic can have stripes or a simple design worked in the front.

OLD SHEPHERD
The basic shape should be in fawn felt or suitable sturdy material. He has long grey hair and a full grey beard, a head-dress of white muslin and a band of blue braid round his head. His tunic is simple decorated in greens, reds and oranges.

YOUNG SHEPHERD
The basic shape should be in fawn felt or suitable sturdy material. He has dark hair and is clean shaven. His head-dress is of white muslin with a rust-coloured braid band. His tunic is decorated in green, rust, black, yellow and white. Woolly lambs made from balls of white wool, fashioned as lambs, could be given to the shepherds to carry, together with staffs.

CASPAR
The basic shape should be in blue felt or other rich material. His tunic has an elaborate design of three rows of yellow ribbon covered with embroidery in red, yellow and white; in between sew bugle beads in white, small beads in yellow and several rows of gaily-coloured beads and embroidery. His head-dress is a linen handkerchief topped by a gold crown encrusted with sequins and brightly-coloured beads.

MELCHIOR
The basic shape should be in black felt or other dark material. His tunic has a design of a row of red ribbon and a row of yellow ribbon; gaily-coloured beads and shiny, green cord couched in a design; gold sequins and white beads and embroidery in gold and white. His head-dress is several layers of wide, yellow silk ribbon hanging down the side of his head to the front of his tunic, topped by a golden turban encrusted with coloured sequins and coloured buttons.

BALTHAZAR
The basic tunic should be of yellow felt or other rich material. His tunic has a design of two rows of emerald green silk ribbon embroidered over in yellow, blue, red and orange, plus a row of gold flower sequins and another row of red sequins tipped with green and red embroidery. The whole effect is bold and colourful. His head-dress is a thin material with a lurex thread running through it to add richness which drapes beautifully. This is topped by a red velvet cap encrusted with gold sequins and coloured beads to represent jewels. Suitable gifts should be made for the kings to carry.

29

Body

Arm

fold

fold

Leg

Foot

CUTHBERT THE CUBE

Materials

Six 10 cm squares of felt—two pink, two blue
*   *and two purple*
Odd scraps of blue and red felt
Black cotton
Two blue sequins
Pink felt for arms
Blue felt for legs
Kapok or old nylon tights for stuffing
Matching cottons

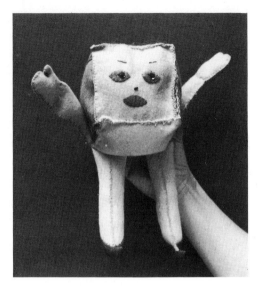

Method

Take one of the 10 cm squares of pink felt and sew on eyes in blue felt with a blue sequin for the iris. Embroider in eyebrows and nose in black cotton and add red felt for the mouth. Blanket stitch all the squares together to form a cube, using matching cotton for the sewing and pairing off colours opposite each other on the cube. Squares may be decorated with embroidery if desired. Leave one seam open and stuff the cube with kapok or chopped up old nylon tights, firmly but carefully keeping the shape of the cube. If you use stranded embroidery cotton for sewing the sides of the cube, three strands will be sufficient. Matching cotton is cheaper and stronger.

Cut two arms in pink felt. Oversew the hand and long seam; stuff hand firmly and sew to secure stuffing. Your thumb and little finger should easily go into the arms to manipulate them with the other three fingers sitting on the top of the cube after the arms have been sewn into position. Cut two legs in blue felt and oversew long seam. Cut two feet in red felt and sew onto legs as shown. Sew legs onto cube as shown.

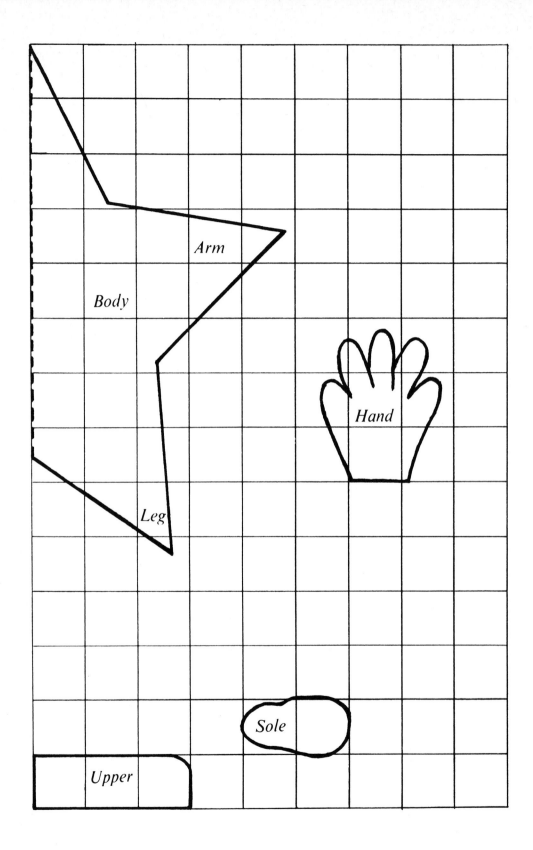

Arm

Body

Hand

Leg

Sole

Upper

SAMMY STAR

Materials

Piece of yellow felt 20 cm square
Scrap of purple felt for shoes
Embroidery silks and sequins
Scraps of pink felt for hands
One bell
Kapok or old nylon tights for stuffing

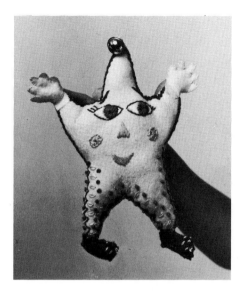

Method

Cut two stars in yellow felt as illustrated. Embroider face as shown and add blue eyes with white surrounds, a brown outline for the eyes and eyelashes and eyebrows, pink cheeks, nose and mouth. Decorate the legs of the star if you wish with embroidery stitches. Sew both pieces of star together, leaving opening for light stuffing, being careful not to lose the shape.

Cut four uppers in purple felt for the shoes. Decorate with green sequins and yellow lazy daisy stitch. Cut two soles. Sew back seam of uppers and toe seam, and then sew uppers onto soles. Stuff firmly and attach into position on the legs of the star as shown.

Cut four hands in flesh pink felt. Sew pieces together leaving opening at wrist. Sew hands onto the arms of the star as shown, leaving the back piece of the wrist felt open for insertion of the little finger and thumb. This allows you to work the puppet with the remaining three fingers tucked in behind. Finally, sew a bell onto the head peak of the star.

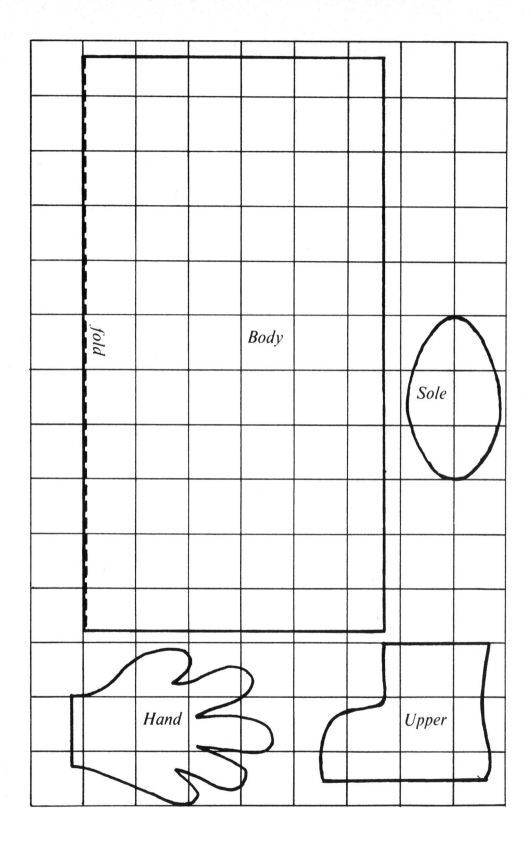

fold

Body

Sole

Hand

Upper

OLGA OBLONG

Materials

Piece of emerald green felt 21 cm square
Black wool or thick embroidery cotton
Scraps of red felt for boots
Scraps of felt for facial features
Oddments of flesh pink felt for hands
Kapok or old nylon tights for stuffing

Method

Cut out the body in green felt. Embroider the bottom half of the oblong (this is the skirt half). Sew on facial features as shown. Make white surrounds to the eyes with blue irises and a red mouth. Work in the hair line with French knots in black wool or thick embroidery thread. Oversew two side seams and stuff lightly with kapok or chopped up nylon tights.

Cut four hands and stitch all round fingers in matching cotton. Sew these onto the body, leaving the back edge of the wrist open. This puppet is manipulated in the same way as the previous one by inserting the little finger and the thumb into the hands. Cut out four uppers and two soles. Stitch uppers together and then onto sole with contrasting cotton or embroidery thread in blanket stitch. Stuff firmly and sew onto oblong as shown.

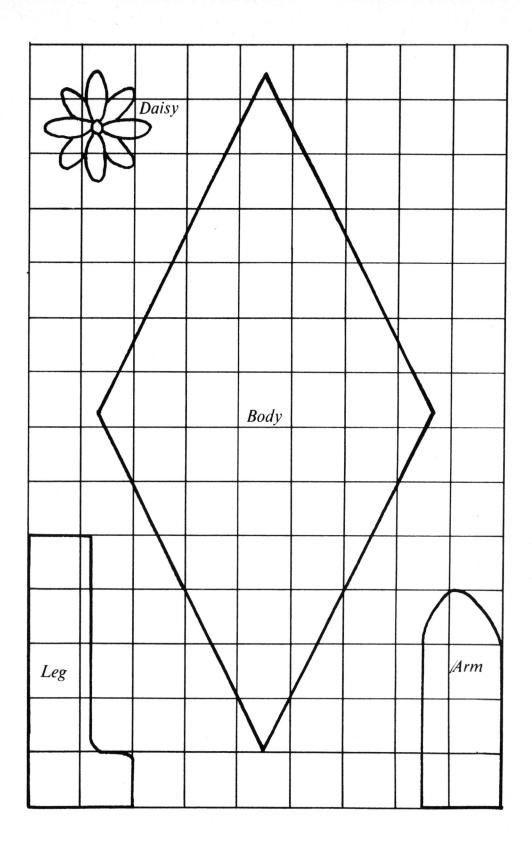

DAISY DIAMOND

Materials

Piece of orange felt 25 cm square
Blue felt for legs
Orange or yellow felt for arms
Scraps of white and yellow felt for daisies
Embroidery cotton for face features
Kapok or old nylon tights for stuffing

Method

Cut two diamond shapes as shown for the body. On the top half of one diamond shape embroider in the face features. Cut out six daisy shapes—petals in white felt, centres in yellow felt. These six daisies will be needed to sew onto the bottom half of the front of the diamonds. Sew or stick the daisies into position.

Cut four arms in orange or yellow felt. Sew the front of the straight edge onto the diamond shape. Leave the back of the straight edge open for the little finger and thumb to manipulate puppet, putting the other three fingers at the back of the diamond.

Cut four legs in blue felt. Embroider with lazy daisy stitch and French knots to match the colour of the diamond. Sew seams, stuff firmly, and stitch onto the diamond shape at the back.

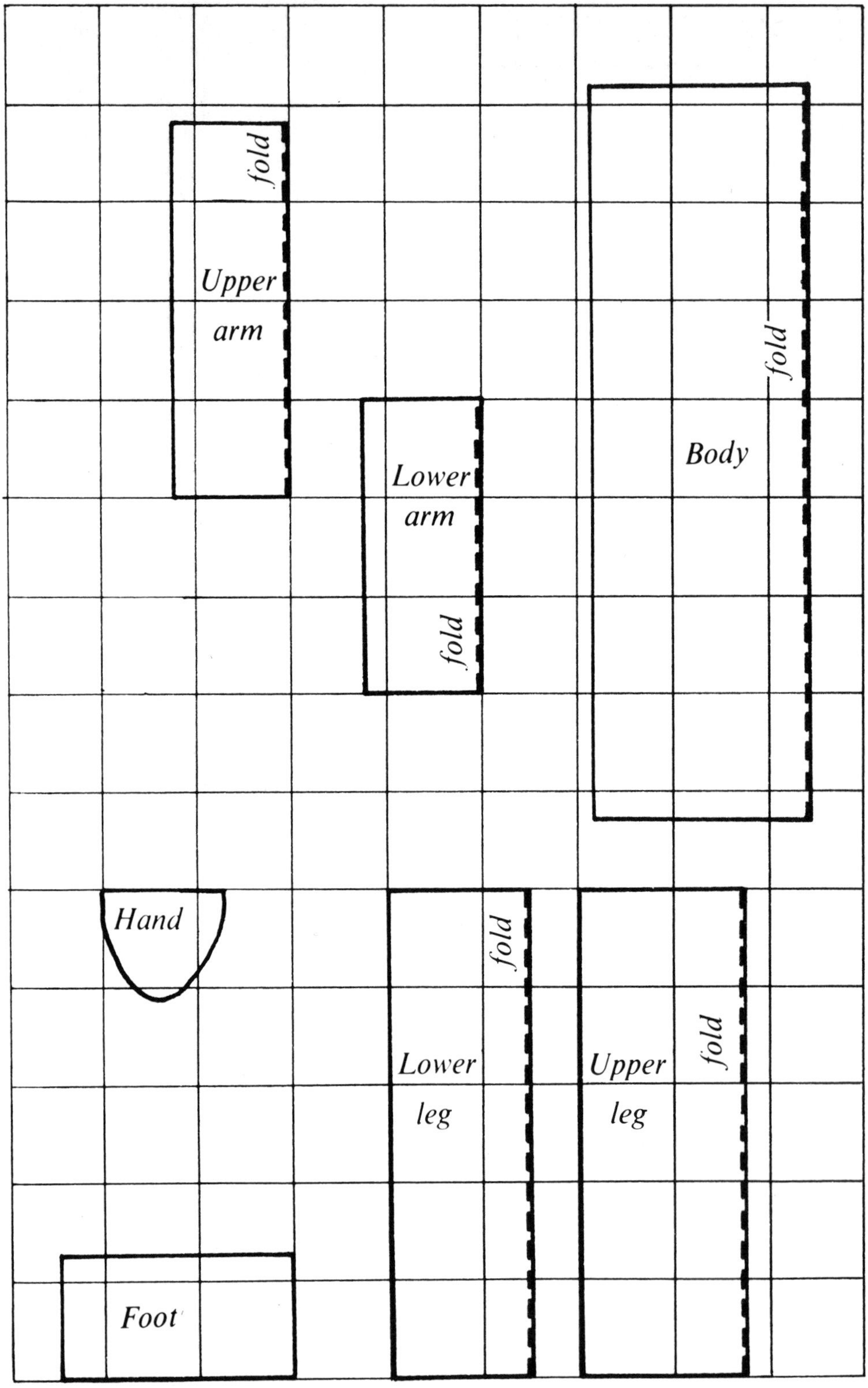

Upper arm *fold*

Lower arm *fold*

Body *fold*

Hand

Lower leg *fold*

Upper leg *fold*

Foot

THE BASIC BODY

Materials

Brown paper or newspaper
Flesh-coloured stout cotton material
Strong thread
Wood and hooks to make holder
Mask (directions on next page)

Method

Newspaper or brown paper tightly rolled makes the filling for the marionette. For the body cut a piece of material 18 cm × 15 cm. Roll up the paper to fill these measurements, then stitch the material firmly round the rolled paper. The legs are made in three pieces and each piece must be formed from rolled and covered paper, tightly sewn to form a sack. The measurements for the upper leg are 7 cm × 10 cm. The lower leg 6 cm × 10 cm and the foot 5 cm × 2.5 cm. Each sack has to be sewn to the next one in such a way that it is flexible and the limb as a whole moves easily, otherwise the marionette will not work well. The arms are made in three pieces; the upper arm measures 5 cm × 7.6 cm, the lower arm 5 cm × 6 cm and the hand is a piece of felt cut as illustrated to fit on the end of the arm. Before the head goes on the marionette measures about 37.5 cm.

The stringing up is as in the diagram. Strong thread should be attached through the knee joints and taken up to each end of the cross bar in the form of the holder. Sew a continuous thread through each hand and pass it through a screw in the front of the wide cross bar; this enables the hands to move up and down. The head has two threads, one on each side, to steady it. These are attached to a screw placed in the centre of the wide bar of wood; the whole marionette is steadied by another thread attached to the back and tied onto the end of the wide piece of wood. The marionette has to be dressed before the stringing can take place.

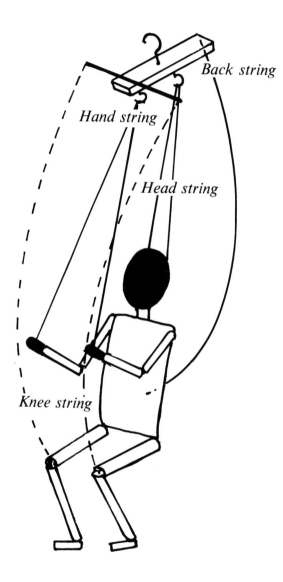

Back string

Hand string

Head string

Knee string

40

THE MASK

Materials

Flesh-coloured stockinette
Tissue paper
Old white sheeting
Plastic doll of right proportions
Vaseline
Polycell paste

Method

Find a cheap plastic doll with the correct head measurements (circumference roughly 20 cm). Length from top of head to neck 10 cm. Mix polycell in cold water, about a heaped teaspoonful to half a cup of water, stir until dissolved and leave to stand for ten minutes. Rub the face and head of the doll with Vaseline to prevent mask from sticking.

Take about a desertspoonful of polycell and rub it thoroughly into the old white cotton which should be large enough to cover the face and the back of the head. Rub it well in until it has formed a coating. Then put it over the face of the doll crossways and gently ease in the nose, eyes, chin, sides of the face and right round to the back of the head. Cover this area with tissue paper. Taking a piece of pink stockinette and, rubbing the polycell in well, spread it carefully over the face, head and neck. Take great care to push in all the crevices and make sure that there are no unnecessary creases in the stockinette. Then leave to dry. (You can do this in an airing cupboard or in the hot sun, or three days at room temperature.)

The shape of the face of the doll you have chosen may be changed by the moulding of the face with plasticine before the mask is made. When the mask is dry, gently peel it off and paint in the features. If you have taken the material carefully to the back of the head, this will be strong enough to take the wig. For the marionettes stuff well with stuffing kapok, chopped up nylon tights or anything suitable. For the nativity hand puppets a space for the fingers must be left, but the head-dress together with the wig will strengthen the back of the head which will be its weakest point.

41

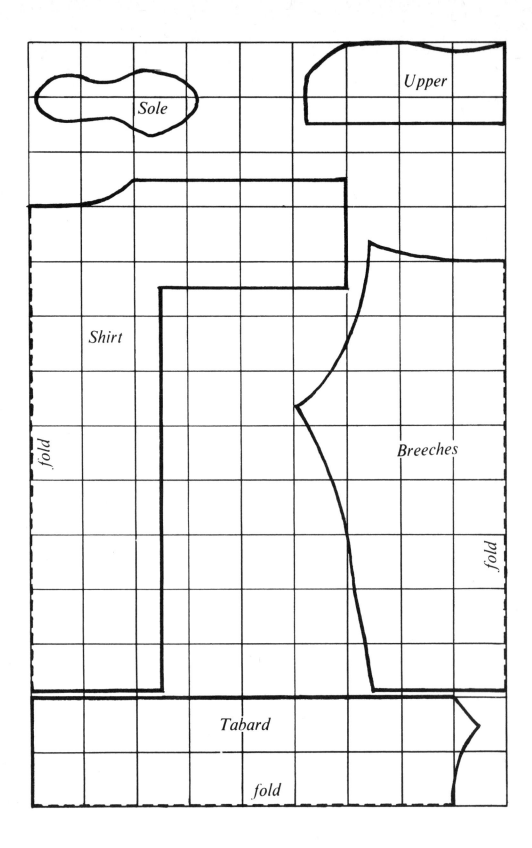

Sole

Upper

Shirt

fold

Breeches

fold

Tabard

fold

MORRIS DANCER (DURHAM RAMS)

Materials

One basic body (see p. 39)
One mask (see p. 41)
Red felt for tabard
Black felt for breeches
White stockinette for stockings
Soft black leather for shoes
Yellow and blue ribbon for decoration
White dishcloth yarn for hat
Bell
Small pebbles or stones to weight shoes
Old handkerchief for shirt and handkerchiefs
Yellow embroidery thread

Method

Put together one basic body and mask. Paint the mask and put a wig of any colour on it. Start with the feet first and work up. Make socks to above the knee in stockinette and sew into position. Cut four uppers and two soles from soft black leather. Sew backs of uppers and attach onto soles. Put on marionette and sew into position, after putting small pebbles in the shoe for weight. Make laces from black cotton and tie in bow.

To make the bells, sew strips of red, yellow and blue ribbon onto another strip of ribbon, adding small beads to represent a bell.** Tie the ribbon round leg under knee and add a piece of cotton tied round calf.

Cut out breeches in black felt and sew where shown as dotted lines on illustration. Sew onto marionette. Make a shirt from white lawn cutting a strip of narrow white ribbon to sew round neck as collar and as cuffs. Put shirt on marionette and tuck into breeches. Cut out tabard in red felt and embroider in yellow the ram's head both on the back and the front. Sew underarm and shoulder seams whilst on the marionette.

Cut two 7.5 cm squares from the white lawn, whip edges and put one in each hand as a handkerchief. Crochet with dishcloth yarn a hat; starting with the crown crochet in half treble until the crown is the size of the marionette's head, then in double crochet continue until the brim is 3.7 cm in diameter. Trim hat with red, blue and yellow ribbons and rosettes. Turn the brim up when finished. Sew a bell under the tabard at the back to make the required sound. Now your Morris Dancer is ready to be strung up.

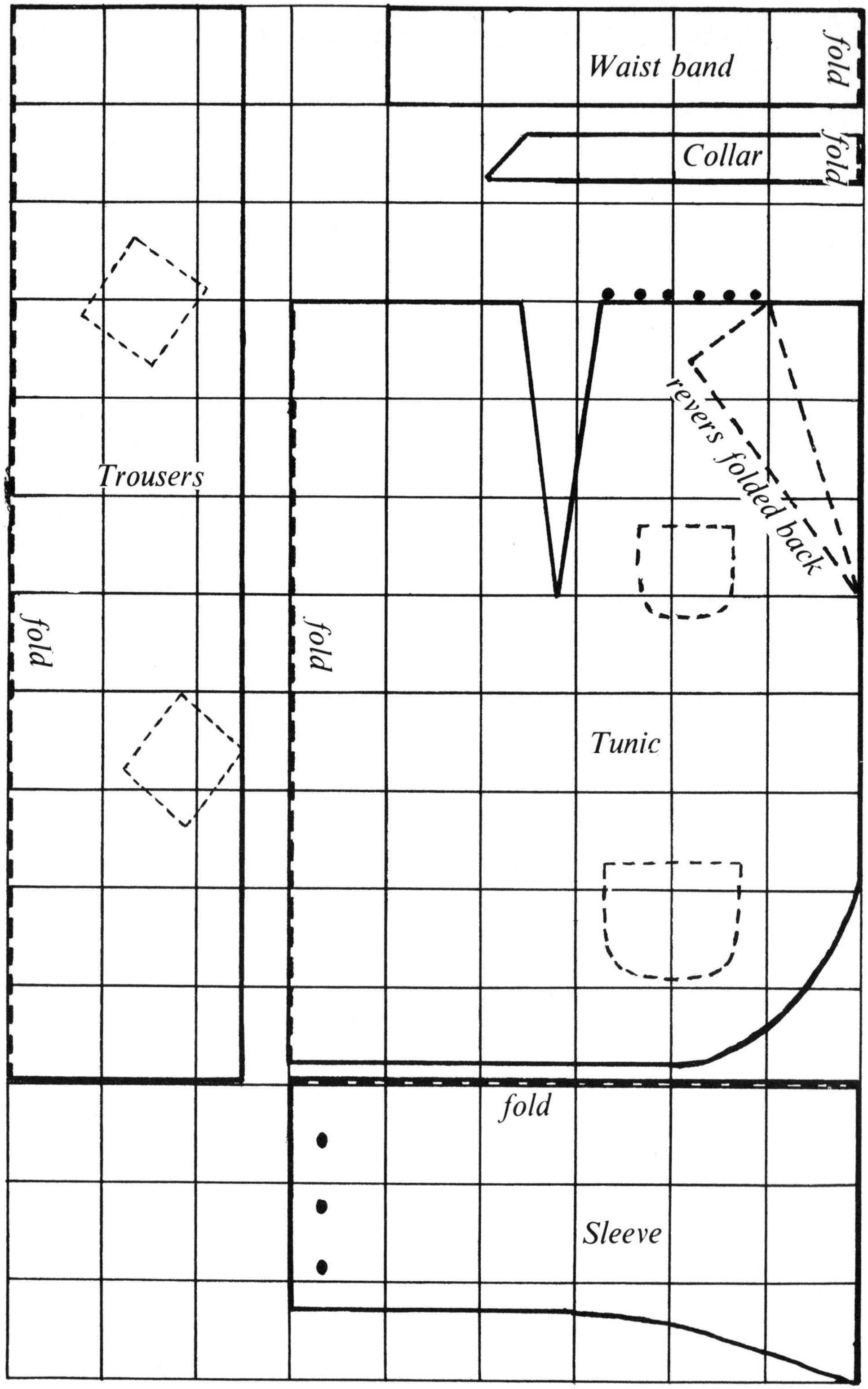

Waist band *fold*

Collar *fold*

revers folded back

Trousers

fold

fold

Tunic

fold

Sleeve

MORRIS DANCER (FOOL)

Materials

One basic body (see p. 39)
One mask (see p. 41)
White felt for trousers
White stockinette for socks
Soft black leather for shoes
Fawn felt for coat
Old handkerchief for shirt
Braid for decoration
Yellow, white and pink embroidery thread
Yellow wool for hat
Narrow green ribbon for rosettes
Red, blue and yellow ribbon for decoration

Method

Follow method for Morris Dancer (Durham Rams) to **.

Cut trousers from white felt. Sew on patches, one in orange and one in yellow, in positions marked with dotted lines. Cut out shirt in white lawn as for Morris Dancer. Cut out collar and sew to shirt. Sew side and shoulder seams of shirt and gather sleeves onto a narrow strip as a cuff. Open the front and sew on small beads as buttons. Put on marionette and sew securely at waist, after tucking into trousers.

Cut out jacket and sleeves in fawn felt. Sew underarm seams then sew on gold or silver beads as buttons where shown, three on each sleeve at the cuff edge. Sew sleeve into jacket. Cut four pockets as shown and, after sewing braid on top, sew them into position on jacket. Embroider rose in white, with pink edges and yellow centre under top right hand pocket of jacket. Sew shoulder seams adding six silver or gold beads to match sleeve on seam. Turn back revers where shown as dotted line, and put on marionette, sewing into correct position. Decorate with braid where shown on jacket.

Using yellow 4-ply wool, crochet in half treble a cap, starting with the top of the crown and continuing until the cap fits the head, coming to just above the eyebrows; make a chain to fasten hat under chin. Make three rosettes with narrow green ribbon and sew one under each side of the revers on the jacket. Sew the third on the crown of the hat. Your Fool is now ready to be strung.

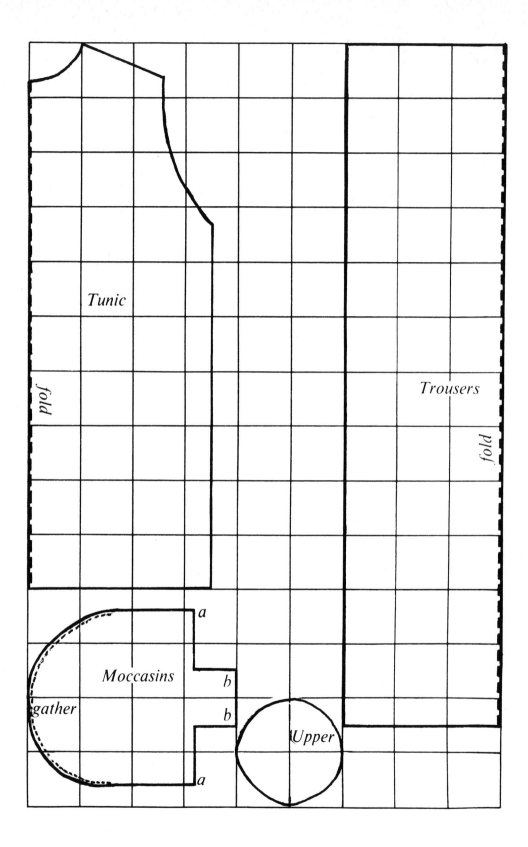

Tunic

fold

Trousers

fold

a

Moccasins

b

b

gather

Upper

a

LOWER WATHA

Materials

One marionette body (see p. 39)
One mask (see p. 41)
Soft but sturdy material for trousers
Soft leather or felt in red for moccasins
Small beads to decorate moccasins
Black wool for hair
Coloured wool to bind hair and fringe tunic
Fawn wool to knit jersey (4-ply)
Small stones or pebbles to weight moccasins
Feather for head-dress
Material for tunic

Method

Join the basic body and the mask together. Paint the mask and attach hair to hang over shoulders on both sides. Measure off sufficient wool to cover the head nicely and stick into position. Then, parting the hair in the middle from the back, bind hair each side of the face for about 1.2 cm with red wool. Paint in the features and stick a feather in the back of the head. Make a plait with about three different colours of wool and tie this round the head Indian fashion.

Cut two pieces of material about 12 cm wide, measuring from the waist to the ankle. Make simple trousers and sew onto marionette at waist. Cut two pieces of tunic material measuring from the shoulder to 4.5 cm below waist. Make this wide enough to fit over the hips of the marionette and taper to fit snugly at the shoulders. When you have made the jersey (see below) fit the tunic and criss-cross red wool down the front to look like an opening. Tie at waist in a bow.

With the fawn wool and a pair of No. 10 needles cast on 30 stitches. Rib for about 2.5 cm (k.1, p.1). Stocking stitch (1 row k, 1 row p) from 1.25 cm below trouser waist line to neck. Cast off and make another piece to match. Make sleeves by casting on 20 stitches and rib for six rows, then change to stocking stitch. Increase at both ends of the row every ten rows and make the sleeve long enough to reach from wrist to where it has to be sewn into the jersey. Put jersey on marionette and sew at neck and waist. Decorate sleeve along seam line by fringing red, orange, blue, yellow and green wool.

Cut two pieces of leather or felt for moccasins. Join seams a–b and gather where illustrated. For the top of the moccasins, cut a circle 4 cm in diameter and decorate with bugle and small beads. Sew onto gathered part of the moccasins and, filling the sole with small stones for weight, sew onto the feet of the marionette.

Plait coloured wool into a tie for the waist; tie round the tunic pulling tight ending in a bow. Then string up the marionette as shown and it is ready to use.

LOWER WATHA'S MAGIC MOCCASINS

Lower Watha has magic red moccasins that can take him anywhere he wants to go. Make up the story as you go along, fitting him in with whatever is the topic of conversation today. He can visit the nearby circus, striding along to see the elephants, the bears and the monkeys; he can manage the trapeze or calm the lions in the cage. He can practise a fire drill with the children, striding through the school ringing the bell to warn the children there is a fire and lead them all to safety. He can join the cricket or football teams of the school and play wonderfully. He can rescue animals from wolves, climb mountains, beat the rapids, or simply do ordinary things like getting up in the morning, going out of his gate and closing it with a bang, walk down the road and practise his green cross drill before crossing. He can swim the river, cross the bridge and climb a tree, or find someone who is lost.

He can be used with any of the other puppets—to help Klintoch find his smile, for instance. He can go on a discovery walk or an environmental walk. He can walk, sit, jump on the spot or lie down; with a little practice he can do anything. He is a favourite in my classroom and the children are always willing to make up adventures for him.